# Aberystwyth

## THE BIARRITZ OF WALES

## OFFICIAL GUIDE AND SOUVENIR

*A facsimile reprint
of the original edition
published in 1924*

Cyflwyniad Hawlfraint / Introduction Copyright © 2015 Cyngor Ceredigion

ISBN: 978-0-9927346-3-3

Cyhoeddwyd gan
Gwasg y Gors, Hafan, Taliesin, Machynlleth, SY20 8JH
ar ran Archifdy Ceredigion

Published by
Gwasg y Gors, Hafan, Taliesin, Machynlleth SY20 8JH
on behalf of Ceredigion Archives

# Rhagarweiniad

Pan ddes i o hyd i gopi gwreiddiol o Aberystwyth, Official Guide and Souvenir mewn siop lyfrau yn Macclesfield meddyliais ar unwaith y dylwn ei brynu a mynd ag ef adref i'w briod le. Ond yn ddiweddar rwyf wedi dod i'r casgliad fod pwy bynnag oedd piau'r llyfr yn siŵr o fod wedi'i drysori am
flynyddoedd lawer fel rhywbeth i gofio am eu gwyliau ar lan y môr yn nhref arbennig Aberystwyth. Holl bwrpas y llyfr oedd ei fod yn gadael y dref!

Gobeithiwn y byddwch chwithau hefyd yn prynu'r ailargraffiad hwn o'r llyfr gwreiddiol a gyhoeddwyd yn y 1920au. Mae rhai o'r manylion yn dal yn berthnasol ac yn ddifyr, ond mewn rhannau mae fel mynd yn ôl mewn amser – wrth ddarllen byddwch yn dychwelyd i Aberystwyth pan oedd y rhifau ffôn yn fyrrach, pan oedd golau trydanol yn dal yn beth newydd yn y gwestai, a phan fyddech wedi talu dau swllt a chwech am botel o bersawr 'Aberystwyth Breezes'.

Helen Palmer
Archifydd y Sir, Archifdy Ceredigion

# Introduction

When I found an original copy of Aberystwyth, Official Guide and Souvenir in a bookshop in Macclesfield my first thought was to buy it and take it home to where it belonged. But more recently I've realised that its previous owners must have cherished it for many years as a lovely souvenir of their sea-side holidays in the very special resort which is Aberystwyth. This is a book which was made to leave town !

We hope you too will buy and enjoy this facsimile reprint of the original 1920s edition. In some respects it's still an interesting guide to the town ; in other respects it's like time travel – for it will transport you back to an Aberystwyth where telephone numbers were still in single figures,  where electric light was still a special feature in the hotels , and where a souvenir bottle of 'Aberystwyth Breezes' perfume would cost you  two shillings and sixpence .

Helen Palmer
County Archivist, Ceredigion Archives

# Belle-Vue Royal Hotel

Occupying the premier position on Sea Front, Modern Appointments, Up-to-Date Sanitation, Excellent Cuisine, :: :: Moderate Tariff. Under personal supervision of Proprietor and Proprietress. Garage, private lock-ups. :: :: :: ::

Telephone No. 39. Telegrams : " Belle-Vue.''
And
Ivy Bush Hotel, Carmarthen. Telephone No. 38.

# LION ROYAL
# HOTEL

### Officially Appointed by the A.A.

### Proprietor : T. CRAVEN

Every consideration given for the comfort
of visitors by the personal supervision
- - of the Proprietors - -
Garage for one hundred cars.

*The Hotel Omnibus meets all trains.*

*Two Billiard Tables.*

Telegrams—
Lion Aberystwyth.

Telephone—
No. 8.

# " *Deva* "

## Private Hotel and Boarding Establishment

### (Also Residential Winter Hotel)

Premier position. Centre of Marine Promenade. Recently reorganised and brought up-to-date. Well furnished rooms. Liberal and well-appointed table

Electric Light throughout

Sanitary arrangements perfect

Under personal management—Mrs. E. Kenrick

# CAERLEON HOUSE

Victoria Marine Terrace : *Proprietress:*
Mrs. HELLABY

CAERLEON BOARDING ESTABLISHMENT, ABERYSTWYTH

| | |
|---|---|
| ON SEA FRONT | OPEN DURING WINTER |
| NEAR LINKS & | |
| TENNIS : : : | BATHS—HOT & COLD |

# CLARENDON
## Boarding Establishment

This Establishment is sheltered from the North and East Winds. Commands excellent view of the Bay on the Marine Parade. Near Golf Links & Tennis Courts

Conducted by Mesdames BUSCH and JACKSON

### Victoria
## Marine Terrace

---

# THE RICHMOND
## BOARDING ESTABLISHMENT

Best Position on Promenade, Excellent Cuisine, highly recommended, Near Golf Links, Tennis Courts and Bowling :: :: Green. :: ::

*Apply for Tariff*, MR. & MRS. R. G. COWERN.

## 44 MARINE TERRACE

11

12

# REA'S
## TERRACE ROAD,
### :: ABERYSTWYTH ::

*Wholesale and Retail*

*Wine & Spirit*

*Merchants* ::

*Restaurateurs.*

## REA'S LOUNGE
———————IS THE———————
## RENDEZVOUS

15

**The British Petrol**

*for* Power
Mileage
Economy
Uniformity
Cleanliness
Easy-Running
Quick-Starting
Any type of Car
On any kind of road

the Best Possible
IS

*The
British
Petrol*

British Petroleum Co. Ltd. 22, Fenchurch St. London E.C. 3.
Distributing Organization of the
ANGLO – PERSIAN OIL CO. LTD.

17

# LEWIS J. MORGAN

THE
## Strand Drapery Stores

DRESSES AND GOWNS AND MEN'S WEAR
MILLINERY, COSTUMES, COATS
HOSIERY, LINGERIE, GLOVES

## Great Darkgate Street (Opposite G.P.O.)
## Aberystwyth

# RICHARDS
## & CO.

### Ladies' & Gentlemen's
# TAILORS

# Outfitters & Hosiers

*BOYS', YOUTHS' & MEN'S
READY-TO-WEAR CLOTH-
ING IN STOCK* :: :: ::

*Also an assortment of TIES, COLLARS,
SHIRTS, PYJAMAS, Etc.*

ALPHA, THETA and WOLSEY
Underwear stocked

---

# 4 and 6 MARKET STREET
## ABERYSTWYTH

# Make a Point of Visiting
## THE
## Expert Master Tailor
## and Complete Outfitter

# Arthur Owen
## -25 North Parade-

Winner in open competition of several
GOLD and SILVER MEDALS and
DIPLOMAS for Excellency in the
Art of HIGH-CLASS TAILORING

SPECIALISTS IN

## LADIES' COSTUMES,
## - COATS, FROCKS, -
## BLOUSES, JUMPERS,
## DRESS MATERIALS,
## Hats, Ribbons, Hosiery.

**LOCAL AGENT FOR**

" CHRISTY'S "
" TRESS " HATS,
" RUMSEY
WELLS " CAPS

" AERTEX '
CLOTHING,
" ELLAN-ESS "
" JAY'S,"
" VIYELLA "
UNDERWEAR

" AQUASCUTUM "
" NICHOLSON'S "
RAINCOATS

An Establishment—Noted for its excellence of
Choice—Charming—Distinctive and Reliable Goods
No connection with any other Firm in the Town.

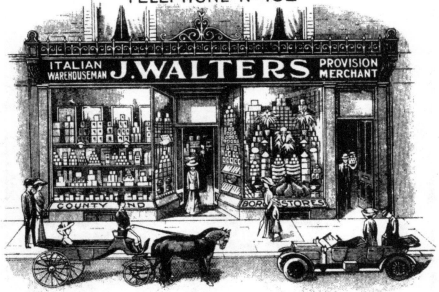

# For Luncheons, Dinners, Teas and Suppers

TRY

# CAFÉ ORIENTAL

*Largest Cafe in the Town.*

*Parties Catered for.  ::  Rooms Reserved.*

—o—

COOKED MEATS of every description.

Up-to-date CONFECTIONERY made on the Premises.

# WARD & CO. LTD.

## High=class Bakers, Cooks, Confectioners and Caterers.

Cafe Oriental and at 38 Great Darkgate St.,
ABERYSTWYTH.

WINE MERCHANTS.                    'Phone 52.

# Go to ASHLEY'S
# COLISEUM CAFÉ
# and RESTAURANT

*Open Daily from* 6.30 *a.m. to* 11 *p.m.*
*Sundays*      ,,      6.30   ,,   ,, 9.30 ,,

Breakfasts, Luncheons and Teas provided on the Shortest Notice. Our Specialities:—Early morning Tea and Coffee, Late Fish Suppers, Quick Service and reasonable Charges. All the Visitors on the Beach are well catered for at Ashley's famous Ice Cream and Refreshment Kiosk, open daily from 6 a.m. till 9 p.m. Tea and Coffee served to Bathers from 6 a.m. Fruit, Chocolate and Sweets, Refreshing Drinks at Popular Prices.

## The ARCADE, Terrace Road,
### Aberystwyth.

# JONES BROS.

## PIONEERS IN THE MOTOR
## :: CHAR-A-BANC TRADE ::

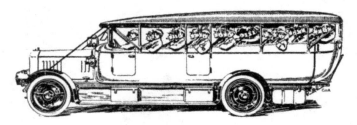

## LOOK OUT FOR
## THE GREY CARS

Leaving Marine Parade Daily 9-30 a.m.
and 2-15 p.m.

Trips arranged to all places of interest, *viz.*:—
Llandrindod Wells, Ellan Valley, Dolgelley,
Talyllyn Lakes, Bettws-y-Coed, Tenby, etc.

## Also Up-To-Date Touring and Closed
## CARS FOR HIRE

Booking Offices : 58 Terrace Rd., and Garage, North Parade

Telephone : No. 49

HEAD OFFICE : GARAGE, NORTH PARADE
Garage Accommodation for 150 cars

# Motor Garage and Engineering Works

# THE WEST WALES GARAGES, LTD.

## NORTH PARADE

## GARAGE OPEN DAY AND NIGHT.

Distributors for the best makes of Cars.

An Up-to-date Engineering Plant for repair of all Motor Vehicles.  ::  ::  ::

Large Stock of Accessories. Private Lock-ups.  Accommodation for 100 Cars.

CARS FOR HIRE.  ::  ::  14-SEATER PNEUMATIC - TYRED  MOTORS  :: WILL RUN TO ALL PARTS DAILY. PRIVATE PARTIES A SPECIALITY.

::  ::  ::  Estimates given.  ::  ::  ::

Telegrams :
"Petrol, Aberystwyth."

Telephone : 111
Aberystwyth.

30

# Central Hotel

## ABERYSTWYTH

 o○○◯◯○o

## Family and Commercial

One minute from Sea—Two
from Station, and Tennis
Courts—Ten from Golf Links.
Home Comforts.    Moderate
——————— Charges ———————

*Tariff on*
*Application*

*Telephone:*
*No.* 10

*Proprietor:* E. LLEWELLIN

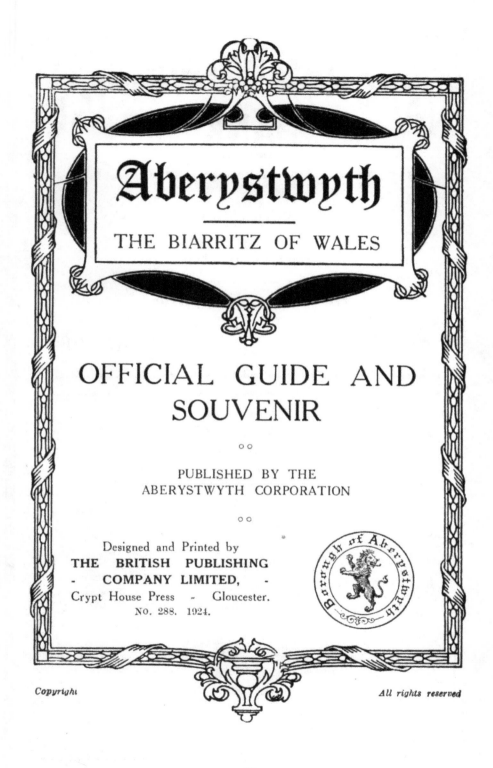

# Aberystwyth

## THE BIARRITZ OF WALES

## OFFICIAL GUIDE AND SOUVENIR

o o

PUBLISHED BY THE
ABERYSTWYTH CORPORATION

o o

Designed and Printed by
**THE   BRITISH   PUBLISHING**
**-   COMPANY   LIMITED,   -**
Crypt House Press   -   Gloucester.
No. 288.   1924.

c

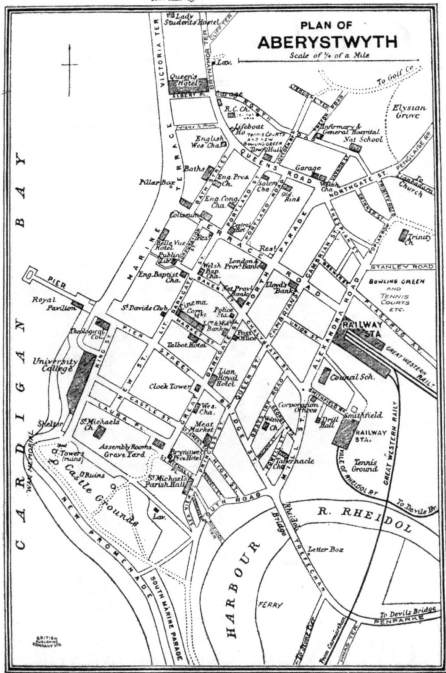

PLAN OF
**ABERYSTWYTH**
Scale of ¼ of a Mile

# *Quality House*

**THIS IS THE PLACE** *where you can be sure of your orders having Prompt Attention*

OWEN'S Specialise in the Production of Dainty Cakes, Fancies, and all High-Class Confectionery, etc., and also in the catering of Wedding Breakfasts, Luncheons, Receptions, At Homes, Dinners, Balls, Picnics, Garden Parties, etc.

If you are on a visit to Aberystwyth you cannot do better than visit OWEN'S for Breakfast, Lunch, Tea or Dinner. They will serve you well and economically

*Confectioners & Caterers*

# OWEN, 19/21 NORTH PARADE

(D. W. TEVIOTDALE) ABERYSTWYTH

*Telegrams : Teviotdale, Aberystwyth*     *Telephone : 32*

*Established* 1815

# . Contents .

38

## FOREWORD.

PROSPECTIVE visitors and residents of Aberystwyth will be saved much vexatious bother on arriving, in endeavouring to discover the best firms with which to deal, if they will consult the select advertisements of traders whose business and other announcements appear in this Guide. All the establishments thus represented are capable of giving their patrons complete satisfaction, and they can be confidently recommended for the courtesy, promptness and careful attention which they will give to any orders entrusted to them.

The traders concerned are quite aware of the fact that they cannot coerce you into placing your orders with them, but they certainly wish you to note that the whole of their resources are at your disposal, both on the grounds of the public spirit that supports local enterprise, and because they feel confident in satisfying your requirements.

The shopping facilities in Aberystwyth deserve full consideration before deciding in favour of any great city's allurements. The prices are low, chiefly owing to the enterprise of the traders, and partly because keen competition has developed the best business instincts and up-to-date methods. Prospective visitors will be bound to be impressed that Aberystwyth is really a high-class shopping centre, even should they only confine their inspections to the window displays of the many high-class shops.

On pages 142 and 143 a short shopping guide and business directory will be found of the traders advertising in this Guide and Souvenir, and visitors and residents alike are confidently asked to verify the accuracy of these statements by patronising the establishments so listed.

To avoid any inconvenience or delay in shopping on arrival, it is respectfully suggested to prospective visitors that their initial orders should be posted a day previous to arrival, when they may have every confidence that the resultant services will justify these recommendations. More especially should this course be adopted when the arrival is on Wednesday, the early closing day in the district.

# INTRODUCTORY.

*" I would detain you here a month or two."*

*The Merchant of Venice.*

 NUGLY ensconced amid a semi-circle of hills, and standing on the shores of Cardigan Bay, is Aberystwyth, to which the proud, but not undeserved, title of the " Biarritz of Wales " has been given.

Cardigan Bay, as a glance at the map will show, occupies practically the whole western seaboard of Wales, and washes the coast lines of Pembrokeshire, Cardiganshire, Merioneth and Carnarvonshire. From its southern point at St. David's Head in Pembrokeshire, to its northern point in Carnarvonshire, and thence to its greatest depth in the centre at Aberystwyth, it makes a magnificent Bay of the Atlantic, containing some fifty square miles of sea.

Welsh tradition says that " Once upon a time " it was a fertile province containing 16 beautiful cities, protected by massive dams, but that Seithenin (described by the Triads as one of the three abandoned drunkards of the Isle of Britain), in a fit of intoxication, let in the waters, and drowned all the inhabitants.

The shape of the Bay itself gives an unusual variety of situation to the various watering places and health resorts on its shores. The southern portion faces east, the middle portion west, and the northern portion south and south-west, but situation and climate, combined with its great natural endowments (supplemented by the enterprise of its public authorities and private inhabitants) have brought Aberystwyth to its present position of being the ideal health and holiday resort, and have rendered it equal to, and not surpassed by, any seaside resort on the coasts of the United Kingdom.

In many respects the main features of Aberystwyth as a health and pleasure resort may be summed up in the following quotation from the *Liverpool Courier :* " Aberystwyth itself is a finely built town with great natural advantages, which have been developed with taste and enterprise by the Corporation. Naturally, the Corporation are anxious that the town shall become better and wider known, even than it is; but though they may be interested, they have a very clear conscience in the matter, for it really does seem that all the nice things that are said about the town are thoroughly deserved.

What are the facts? These—'healthful situation, western aspect, picturesque bay, bold open sea; bracing sea and mountain air; gravelly subsoil; sheltered position; romantic and beautiful adjoining country of hill, valley and mountain; excellent centre for outings and excursions; interesting beach, imposing cliff scenery; pure sea water; facilities for bathing; means of entertainment; fine promenade; romantic castle and grounds; abundant hotel, boarding and lodging-house accommodation; good shops, cheap provisions; high record of sunshine, low rainfall, absence of fog, snow and frost; perfect sanitation and an abundance of the purest water in the kingdom.' What more could be required or desired? I have been to Aberystwyth and seen for myself, and I know that there is no exaggeration in the statement."

Portion of Harbour.

Aberystwyth, as a health and pleasure resort, affords as thorough a change in language and nationality, climate and scenery, custom and tradition, as any foreign resort, and is easily accessible from all parts of Great Britain. The late Dr. Murray, of Oxford, the lexicographer, who spoke from experience as a frequent visitor to the West Welsh Coast, bore testimony to these special attractions for English residents. " I confess," he said, " that the beauties of Aberystwyth are exceedingly great, and that the beauties of Wales are very great indeed. Wales is close at hand to England and has advantages which are not to be found in English inland resorts, in Scotland, in the Lake districts, or even in Switzerland. Wales, and Aberystwyth in particular, have the exceptional advantages of a delightful combination of sea and mountain, so that if one has a large family some members of it may like to dabble on the sands while other members may like to ramble over highland, moor and mountain. Aberystwyth has a magnificent sea, sunsets incomparable and a magnificent mountainous hinterland, and all those grand features of nature which, after all, have the strongest influence upon the mind and are our greatest educators."

That testimony of the eminent lexicographer has been confirmed by the experience of hundreds of other visitors qualified to speak with authority after seeing other resorts at home and abroad. A writer to a magazine adds his testimony in the following words : " Aberystwyth, unlike many more tiny resorts in Wales, is still Welsh to the core. The great charm of a Welsh watering place is its combination of home comforts and foreign appearance. At the cost of a small journey—without danger of accident or the discomforts of sea sickness—the tourist is in what is practically a foreign country. Language, faces, worship, scenery, all is delightfully new and strange. Aberystwyth is more than a mere watering place. It is a great educational centre, with its three colleges, and is also the market place of the western slopes of Plimlymon, and this brings into its streets throngs of students as well as country people, whose smiling faces and vivacious demeanour and native speech and knowledge of English, strike the English visitor as something entirely foreign. And, when one comes to think of it, what a delightful variety there still exists, in spite of all prosaic powers working for dead uniformity in these islands of ours. If you ask me where most Welsh characteristics are seen—religious fervour, good Welsh, sincere hospitality, even the old native costume—I would answer that they are best seen at Aberystwyth. For breezy headlands overlooking a glorious expanse of sea, for gorse that seems to glow and burn, for mountain solitudes, for invigorating air, for alternation of stormy height and sheltered valley, give me Aberystwyth of all places in the world."

*Photo—Culliford.*

Portion of Sea Front.

A portion of the South Parade, Aberystwyth.

# AN ANCIENT BOROUGH.

THE discovery a few years ago of an ancient flint weapon factory at the foot of Pen Dinas, which rises to 413 feet on the south side of the town, as well as earthworks on the hill itself, indicates that Aberystwyth was a place of some importance in Neolithic times, when workers fashioned into weapons flints  found on the beach, brought thither from the North of Scotland in the great Ice Age. An interesting collection of these flint weapons is exhibited in the Museum of the College. There was also, in all probability, a fortress at Aberystwyth in the days of the old Welsh tribes. The town, however, owes its origin as a royal borough, to Edward I who erected a castle on a promontory overlooking the sea, granted a charter making the place a trading and municipal centre, and allowed the inhabitants to construct walls and fosses for their protection. Thus Aberystwyth had its Mayor and Corporation officials from early Norman times, and still possesses records of the quaint doings of its Court Leet, when stocks and whipping posts and ducking stools, as well as gallows, were the necessary equipments of a well-found borough. The Castle was dismantled after the Civil War, but the ruins are there to-day to testify to the former magnificence of the fortress. The line of the town walls is still preserved in streets, but the walls have entirely disappeared and are only memorialised in the names of Great Darkgate and Little Darkgate Streets. During the reign of Charles I, Bushel, who farmed the royal mines of Cardiganshire, was allowed to establish a mint in the Castle for the coinage of silver found in the lead. He subsequently lent his royal patron £40,000 and defrayed the cost of clothing the King's army. A set of these coins is also in the College Museum, and old stone and iron balls used in the various sieges to which the Castle was subjected in former days, with other relics found during excavation, are exhibited at the Public Library. The Castle Grounds are now vested in the Town Council, which has intersected them with walks and provided seats commanding charming views of Cardigan Bay and its background of mountains.

Castle Grounds and War Memorial. Fleet in the background.

In the courtyard of the Castle is a Druidic circle, formed of huge stone blocks, contributed by each of the twelve counties, with an inscription in old Welsh " coelbren y beirdd," which, though of modern construction, is interesting as illustrating Druidic astronomical worship. On the seaward extremity of the Promontory Aberystwyth has erected a magnificent memorial to its 200 men lost in the war on sea and land. The memorial stands 82 feet high, was designed by Signor Rutteli, cost £7,000, and is surmounted by the Angel of Peace with a figure on the pediment embodying the idea of Humanity emerging from the entanglements of war.

## NATURE'S HEALTH RESORT.

ABERYSTWYTH is one of the oldest, if not the oldest, watering place and health resort in Wales, and owes its origin as such, not to any " development scheme " by enterprising speculators, but to the discovery more than two centuries ago by visitors themselves of the bracing salubrity of its climate, the beauty of its Bay and neighbourhood, the salinity and clearness of the sea water, and the mental and physical recuperative value of the change of scene and circumstance which even a brief visit affords. In those early days English physicians had not acquired the habit of patronising foreign spas and recommending patients to go abroad for what they can well obtain at home, taking millions of money out of the country for which there is no economic return. Thus, Sir James Clark, Sir Astley Cooper, and other eminent members of the medical profession were visitors to Aberystwyth. Sir James Clark, in fact, not only patronised Aberystwyth, but gave it as his opinion, from his personal experience, " that a fortnight's stay at Aberystwyth will do as much good as a month's stay at most other watering places. The pure air, its bracing effects, and the extreme change," he adds, " often conduce to feelings of depression and extra debility for the first two or three days, but the medical profession accept this as evidence of speedy and favourable reaction." J. M. W. Turner, also, was a visitor to Aberystwyth, where he transferred to canvas some of its glorious sunset effects.

*Photo—Culliford.*

War Memorial, Aberystwyth.

# PROGRESS AS A WATERING PLACE.

AT the beginning of the eighteenth century Aberystwyth was primarily a sea port with a larger register of shipping than that of Cardiff in those days, a place for ship-building, the centre of a rich lead-mining country, and the outlet for produce of a wide agricultural district. With the advent of railways and the finding of richer deposits of lead elsewhere, the shipping and mining industries declined. In those days the town was mainly confined within the area of the old walls outside of which existed sand dunes on the sea front and a stretch of waste land to the limits of the borough boundary. Fortunately, the old Court Leet had maintained public rights in those waste lands, so when an increasing number of visitors found their way to these shores, parcels of land were leased by the Court Leet for building purposes, and the main streets of the old Norman borough were continued and a well-laid-out town resulted. A fine crescent of hotels, boarding and apartment houses sprung up on the sea front, as well as many houses affording accommodation for visitors in the off streets ; a sea wall was constructed ; a paved promenade of a mile-and-a-half eventually formed ; a sewerage scheme carried out, and an abundant supply of water of the purest quality obtained from a natural lake on Plimlymon Mountain. Private enterprise provided a promenade, pier and pavilion, wherein first-class entertainments are given throughout the year, as well as a Coliseum, the boards of which are frequently occupied by London theatrical companies; a commodious Parish Hall for meetings and various entertainments ; and a large College Hall in which high-class concerts are given throughout the winter months by students of the University School of Music and well-known professionals, under the direction of Dr. Sir Walford Davies. During the season variety entertainments are given in these pavilions. A few years ago the Marine Promenade was extended around the Castle Promontory connecting with the South Marine Promenade. As the extended promenade rises many feet above the foreshore, and the sea, at high tide, against the wall, and at low tide never recedes beyond a couple of hundred feet, promenaders receive the benefit of discharges of positive electricity, which Prince Krapotkin declares are invaluable in cases of nervous debility. The normal population of the borough is between 11,000 and 12,000, increased to some 20,000 during the height of the summer season. The usual provision on the two beaches is made for sea bathing and boats.

Band playing on Castle Grounds.

Portion of South Parade.   Castle and War Memorial.

# THE ATHENS OF WALES.

EVER since the days of Owain Glendwr, in the fourteenth century, Welsh patriots dreamed of a University for Wales, but the dream did not materialise until the early seventies of the nineteenth century, when it assumed concrete form by the purchase of palatial buildings facing the sea at Aberystwyth, originally intended for a monster hotel. The College opened its doors to youth of both sexes and of all creeds and classes in the year 1872, and after a heroic struggle for existence on voluntary contributions ultimately received a Government grant and became a constituent college in the University of Wales. Since then a Theological College has been opened at Aberystwyth for the training of Ministers of the Calvinistic Methodist Church of Wales, and in 1922 the Catholics removed their College from Holywell and opened St. Mary's College on the hillside at Aberystwyth. During the College terms there are, therefore, about 1,000 students receiving training at Aberystwyth, in addition to pupils of private schools for boys and girls, the Convent School, and the County Intermediate Dual School at Ardwyn. During the general scholastic vacation a summer school is held at the College, which is largely attended by educationists from all parts of the kingdom, and during the winter months, when students and pupils keep the town from that stagnation which affects purely summer resorts, in addition to weekly concerts by the College School of Music, College lectures are frequently given by men of special knowledge, to which visitors are welcomed. The Museum at the College, designed to illustrate the archæology, geology and zoology of Wales, as well as the College itself, is thrown open to the public on certain days of the week during the summer vacation. Standing on a hill on the outskirts of the town is the National Library of Wales, which contains many of the Welsh ancient MSS., a rare edition of Chaucer, and thousands of volumes formerly belonging to curious collectors, as well as copies of modern publications under the Copyright Act. The building, which is not yet complete, cost over £100,000. During the summer visiting season an exhibition of paintings is arranged, which is open to the public as is the Library throughout the year. The writer already quoted, referring to Aberystwyth as an educational centre, says : " The University College of Wales at Aberystwyth is one of the finest buildings in Wales, and I say without hesitation, that, as far as health and surroundings are concerned, it is one of the most desirable places for reading in the world. I know students," the writer adds, " who read for sixteen hours a

1.  College Central Hall.     2.  College Museum.

day at Aberystwyth, and through every third night, without losing any of the freshness and grip of their mind." In addition to private libraries, some 10,000 books in the Public Library in Alfred Place are available to visitors at a nominal loan fee, and the Reading Room of the institution is open to non-residents.

## WALKS, OUTINGS AND TOURS.

IT is advisable for the newly-arrived visitor to spend the first few days in acclimatising himself to the change of air and accustomed living by lounging on the beach, for which

The Road to the Golf Links.

purpose abundant chairs are provided, by inspecting the well-stocked shops in the business parts of the town, by listening to the strains of the Municipal Band, by promenading along the sea front, by basking in the sunshine under Craiglais Cliffs, or by visiting the Castle Grounds and ruins in a walk of a few minutes only from any part of the town. The rocky promontory on which the ruin stands runs well out to sea at a considerable altitude, and commands the full extent of Cardigan Bay, from Bardsey Island on the north to Strumble Head in the south, with a fine panorama of mountains for backgrounds, including Snowdon and Cader Idris in Carnarvonshire and Merioneth, and the Precelley Hills in Pembrokeshire. After two or three days of sweet idleness exploration of the immediate country can be made, with beneficial health effects and pleasing sensations to the eye and brain.    North of the Promenade rises to nearly 500 feet Constitution Hill, the summit of which can be reached in a few minutes, and south of the town Pen Dinas, rising to over 400 feet, can be walked in half-an-hour.    Both hills command extensive views. During the season a small railway runs to the summit of Constitution Hill, which has been laid out in Cliff Gardens.    Thence a walk over the cliffs leads, in less than a mile, to the Bay of Clarach and its fine and safe bathing sands, and may be extended by four miles along the cliffs to Borth, where the return journey may be made by train.    Crossing the Harbour by ferry, the stone pier

Trefechan  Bridge  from  the  Harbour.

can be visited, and the walk extended either to the Alltwen Cliffs or along the banks of Ystwyth to Rhydyfelin, returning by the main road.    In a mile-and-a-quarter the sixth-century church, founded by Padarn, at Llanbadarn, which in his days became the centre of an episcopal see, can be visited, and interesting early Christian carved stones in the interior inspected, the return walk being made along the banks of the Rheidol.    In a few minutes from the Promenade the Elysian Grove can be reached, with its enchanting glades and elevated paths and extensive landscape views.    Cwm Woods is a favourite resort of visitors.    In a walk of about a mile, commencing near the side of the Infirmary and edging the golf links, the path reaches an eminence from which, on a clear day, can be seen the three chief mountains of Wales— Plimlymon,  Cader  Idris  and  Snowdon.    Embosomed  in  the woods is Cwm House, where Keble composed the later portions of the *Christian Year*, and where Isaac Williams, the Poet and Hymnist, one of the leaders of the Oxford movement and a friend of Keble, was born, and in the picturesque church of Llangorwen, in the valley below, is a lectern given by him. Directions for many other short walks out of Aberystwyth will be found in local guide books.

The provision of well-appointed motor char-a-bancs and arrangements for concerted tours have made long-distance tours to places of beauty and interest not only possible but easy and pleasant. Motor and other char-a-bancs assemble on the Promenade morning and afternoon for circular tours to the Devil's Bridge, returning through Ponterwyd ; to Birmingham Water Works in the Ellan Valley ; to Corris and Talyllyn Lake, returning round the eastern spur of Cader Idris through Dolgelley, and the coast towns of Merioneth ; to Aberayron and New Quay along a delightful coast road ; to the Llyfnant and Artists' Valleys ; and to the base of Plimlymon at Steddfa Gurig, when an ascent of the mountain may be made in a little over two miles, and an extensive view can be obtained embracing the whole expanse of Cardigan Bay and portions of Shropshire and Hereford, and nearly all the counties of Wales.

The three railways which have their terminus at Aberystwyth also provide exceptional facilities for visiting places of interest in the neighbourhood. By the G.W.R., running eastward, may be comfortably visited the village of Llandre and its quaint hillside churchyard and a well-preserved motte and bailey fortification, returning along the cliffs from Wallog ; Borth with its firm sands ; Ynyslas, with its fantastic sand dunes and shell-strewn beach ; Glandyfi, with its approaches to the lovely valleys of Llyfnant Einion ; Machynlleth and Corris, Talyllyn and Cader Idris, arrangements being made with the toy railway and motor service by which visitors can leave Aberystwyth in the morning, ascend Cader Idris, the most beautiful of all the Welsh mountains, and return home in the evening in time for tea or late dinner. A mountain railway through the Rheidol Valley, which reaches an altitude of 700 feet, opens up by an hour's panoramic run the romantic and enchanting Devil's Bridge district with its glens and gorges, magnificent cascade, wood, river and mountain scenery. By the G.W.R., running south, may be easily visited Llanilar and its quaint church ; Crosswood, the seat of the Earls of Lisburne, and in the locality a well-preserved Neolithic caer and garth ; Strata Florida, for the ruins of its Cistercian Abbey, and the Teify Lakes ; Tregaron, the birth-place of Henry Richard, the apostle of Peace ; and Lampeter, the seat of St. David's

Devil's Bridge, Aberystwyth.

College, returning by the Lampeter–Aberayron railway to Aberayron, and thence into Aberystwyth by G.W.R. motor bus. A
motor run through charming scenery may be made from Aberystwyth up the Valley of the Ystwyth to Pontrhydygroes, whence
a walk may be made through Hafod grounds to the church, which
contains one of Chantrey's masterpieces.

## DEVIL'S BRIDGE AND RHEIDOL VALLEY.

A MOTOR CHAR-A-BANC DRIVE along the southern side
of the Rheidol Valley, ascending to nearly 1,000 feet
above the sea at Aberystwyth, or an hour's train ride on
the Vale of Rheidol narrow-guage mountain railway, takes the
visitor through a charming valley, and lands him at the Devil's
Bridge in the midst of scenery unsurpassed in Wales or anywhere
in the kingdom. Varied, extensive, and charming as are the
views all along the valley, the scenery at the Bridge defeats the
photographer and defies description, though Wordsworth
attempted it :—

> How art thou named ?   In search of what strange land ;
> From what such height descending ?
> Can such force
> Of waters issue from a British source,
> Or hath not Pindus fed thee, where the band
> Of patriots scoop their freedom out with hand
> Desperate as thine ?   Or come the incessant shocks
> From the young spring that smites the throbbing rocks
> Of Via Mala ?   There I seem to stand,
> As in life's morn, permitted to behold
> From the dead chasm woods climbing above woods
> In pomp that fades not.

" Peter Lombard," writing to the *Church Times*, said :   " Of
course, I have seen waterfalls without number in other countries,
but I was not prepared for the beauty of that at Devil's Bridge.
I certainly have never seen a more beautiful fall. It was a
sight of beauty I shall never forget." The River Rheidol, cleav-
ing its way through rocky gorges, opens out in a deep glen into
which tumbles the Mynach Cascade in a broken descent of over
300 feet. Before making its descent, the Mynach has made a
narrow gorge through the rocks and scooped out a gloomy chasm
known as the Devil's Punch Bowl. One hundred and fourteen
feet above the Punch Bowl, where the torrent seethes and swirls
with awful force, the monks of the adjacent abbey of Strata
Florida in the time of Rufus threw a bridge. This was known
to the locality as the Monk's Bridge until a stranger to the Welsh
language came along and not only translated Pont-ar-Mynach
into Devil's Bridge, but attached to it the legend that the devil

constructed it to enable Megan Llandunach to recover her cow which had strayed across the ravine. The condition was that the devil was to have the first living thing that crossed over the bridge. Megan threw a crust of bread over, and, her dog going after it—

> The Devil looked queer and scratched his right ear,
> And sprang from the side of the ravine,
> He exclaimed, "A fine hit; the Devil is bit,
> For the mangy cur isn't worth having."

## THE ADVANTAGES OF ABERYSTWYTH AS A WINTER RESORT.

DURING the Great War thousands of British subjects were denied the privilege of wintering abroad, and had to seek favourable spots within the British Isles. Many solicited the guidance of their medical attendant, who undertook the responsibility of recommending places which offered the most favourable climatic conditions, with the result that those who had for years escaped from what they called the rigours of our winter climate, realised that there was no necessity to leave our shores in quest of health, whilst our seaside and inland health resorts provided the elements and conditions essential for prolonging life, promoting health and preventing disease, and were as abundant within the British Isles, if not more so, than in any other part of the world, with the advantage of home comforts, surroundings and pleasant associations, which are so incorporated with the life of an Englishman. Unfortunately very few facts having been recorded to justify the claims of our winter resorts, we are therefore heavily handicapped in making a selection. Practically every seaside and inland resort in the United Kingdom has been eulogised by the faculty, as well as by the Press, but eulogy unsupported by specific facts is worthless and often misleading. Hence the necessity of promulgating the special features and claims which each individual place is entitled to.

Sir Astley Cooper, Sir Thomas Watson, Sir James Clark, Sir Samuel Wilks, and a host of others have assigned to Aberystwyth top place amongst seaside resorts, and though other places have received similar testimony from eminent medical men [and as a matter of fact these places have much in common] however that might be, the time has arrived for establishing by facts the advantages which our health resorts offer for winter residence, and with that object in view, I shall endeavour to make clear the supreme claims of Aberystwyth.

Situated on the coast of Cardigan Bay, it is open to the bracing and temperate breezes, which blow over the Western Ocean, cool in summer, warm in winter, and exceptionally free from vicissitudes of temperature. Sheltered from the cold north and east winds, the town enjoys practically complete immunity from frost, snow and fogs. The rainfall is low, the percentage of sunshine high, the water supply is exceptionally good, and there are no rivers carrying with them the sewage of large towns to pollute and adulterate the briny quality of the sea, neither are there any factories to foul the air; these conditions

Craiglais, Aberystwyth.

support to a great extent the claims of Aberystwyth as a health resort ; but there are other and exceptional conditions which contribute immensely to its health-giving properties and entitle it to a place of its own—conditions due to its position at the western base of the great mountains of Wales (see map) from which it receives a supply of pure mountain air, which mingles freely with the sea air, forming a blend congenial to those in health as well as to invalids. When the wind is blowing from the sea it makes its presence known far inland by depositing its saline particles on the windows, whilst when blowing from the east, the mountain breezes reveal their presence by the occasional downfall, during the coldest days of winter, of a few hailstones or snow-flakes. It is to this mixture of sea and mountain air, which is maintained in a high state of purity by the restless and alternating currents, " which chase each other in glee, year in and year out," that Aberystwyth is indebted for its remedial agents, which combine the salubrious climatic resources of inland and sea-side resorts—in common phraseology it provides both " bread and cheese," and it should be remembered that these ozone-laden breezes are even more invigorating in winter than in summer, whilst the sheltering hills ensure complete immunity from the trying effects of unrestrained north and east winds.

Aberystwyth is blessed with another munificent gift of nature,

Catching Sprats on Pier Rocks.

which has been overlooked, viz., the hour of sunset, which in addition to the splendour of its radiant rays, furnishes an extension of evening light for 23 minutes beyond what is enjoyed by London and other places similarly situated, and still more so when compared with places further east. This is of considerable advantage during the short days of winter. The geographical position which furnishes this advantage also accounts for the alternating mild and stimulating atmospheric influences, which are provided by the constant mingling of the sea and mountain breezes and to which the regenerating powers of our health resort are greatly attributable.

In the year 1879, Major Tulloch, R.E., Chief Engineer to the Local Government Board, said in his report to the Board, that

" Aberystwyth is possessed of advantages that should make it a popular seaside resort in both summer and *winter ;* it is sheltered from the east and north winds, stands on a porous subsoil, and has some of the finest scenery in the country within a short distance.

The general appearance of the surrounding scenery reminds one not a little of Matthew Arnold's well-known words :—

"Far from Hence
The Adriatic breaks in a warm Bay,
Among the green Illyrian hills, and there
The sunshine in the happy glens is fair,
And by the sea, and in the brakes,
The grass is cool, the sea-side air
Buoyant and fresh, the mountain flowers
More virginal and sweet than ours."

## SANITATION AND WATER SUPPLY.

THE Corporation may truly be said to have a lively sense of their responsibility as hosts to thousands of visitors, and have shown it in practical form by equipping the place with up-to-date sanitary requirements at a cost of at least £200,000, so as to make their town, like Cæsar's wife, above suspicion. An efficient water-carriage system of sewerage has been taken through every part of the town and ventilated according to plans of expert sanitary engineers, the effluent being carried far out to sea by the combined forces of two rivers at a satisfactory distance away from any dwelling.

The other essential of a health resort—water supply— has been provided at a cost of £20,000 in obtaining from Plimlymon Mountain an abundant supply of the purest water it is possible to obtain. It cannot, in fact, be other than pure, for the source is in a natural lake on Plimlymon, 2,000 feet above the sea, high above any human habitation, and the water can be used without filtration for purposes for which distilled water is generally required. This magnificent supply was constructed along the eighteen miles to the source at an original cost of about £1,000 a mile, making it one of the cheapest schemes of water supply on record. In addition to efficient sewerage and water supply, the Corporation, by their Medical Officer and Sanitary Inspector, are vigilant in the prevention of insanitary conditions. The " Notification of Diseases Act " has been adopted, as well as the " Dairies and Milkshops Order," and any outbreak of zymotic disease— or imported case of infection is and has been isolated and successfully checked. The Corporation possess an excellent Isolation Hospital of 16 beds for the treatment and isolation of the general

Upper Falls, Devil's Bridge, Aberystwyth.

infectious diseases, also a well isolated residence known as Alltglaise, about 2½ miles distant from the town, ready for use at any moment in case of an outbreak of small pox.

## METEOROLOGICAL STATISTICS.

THE following statistics are based upon the average *daily* readings taken during a period of twenty years (Aberystwyth being a Meteorological Station) from 1901 to 1920 :—

Dry bulb temperature    50.2
Maximum temperature    54.1
Minimum temperature    45.0
Range of temperature    9.3
Mean temperature    50.0

The average number of frosty days in the year for that period was 20 ; sunless days 60 ; average annual rainfall at the Castle gauge 30 inches ; and the average annual hours of bright sunshine 1,500.

The following comparative statistics for the year 1921 are taken from the report of Joseph Baxendell, Esq., F.R.Met.Soc., Meteorologist to the Southport Corporation :—

| Stations. | Mean Temperature. | | | Mean daily range of Temp. | Total rain-fall inches. | No. of days with 1 m.m. of rain or more | Sun-shine. hrs. |
|---|---|---|---|---|---|---|---|
| | The year | Jan. and Feb. | July and Aug. | | | | |
| Scarborough ... | ... 51.4 | 43.8 | 60.9 | 11.4 | 18.72 | 97 | 1,560 |
| Morecambe ... | ... 50.9 | 42.5 | 61.9 | 11.1 | 33.35 | 140 | 1,682 |
| Blackpool ... | ... 50.7 | 43.3 | 61.0 | 10.9 | 29.68 | 134 | 1,661 |
| Llandudno ... | ... 51.5 | 45.1 | 61.1 | 11.0 | 25.05 | 119 | 1,657 |
| Aberystwyth ... | ... 51.8 | 44.6 | 61.9 | 9.9 | 26.58 | 122 | 1,729 |
| Harrogate ... | ... 48.9 | 41.1 | 59.6 | 13.4 | 23.59 | 111 | 1,546 |
| Leamington Spa | ... 50.9 | 42.8 | 63.0 | 16.8 | 15.30 | 90 | 1,632 |
| Malvern ... | ... 52.0 | 43.5 | 63.9 | 13.3 | 18.53 | 94 | 1,773 |
| Bath ... ... | ... 52.4 | 44.3 | 64.4 | 15.7 | 17.29 | 99 | 1,615 |
| Weston-super-Mare | ... 53.2 | 44.7 | 65.0 | 13.3 | 19.96 | 109 | 1,752 |
| Ilfracombe ... | ... 53.8 | 46.8 | 63.4 | 8.6 | 25.31 | 122 | 1,821 |

The marked feature of these climatological observations is the remarkable evenness of temperature at Aberystwyth throughout the year.

Other features are the amount of the annual sunshine, the absence of fog and the small number of frosty days. Snow seldom falls and when it does it almost immediately disappears. These facts prove that Aberystwyth is climatologically well favoured, and its claims as a health resort, and especially as a place of winter residence, are well substantiated.

1. The Town Hall.   2. A rough sea.
3. The Harbour.   4. College Entrance.

*Photo—Culliford*

Portion of Clarach Beach.

*Photo—Culliford*

Walk on Constitution Hill.

## CORRIS, TALYLLYN LAKE AND CADER IDRIS
### Via Corris Railway.

FROM Aberystwyth a very pleasant excursion, giving a really wonderful variety of magnificent scenery, may be made by taking train to Machynlleth, and changing there to the narrow gauge line of the Corris Railway Company. Machynlleth is the starting point of the Corris Railway, and the commencement of the beautiful scenery which extends right

Talyllyn Lake and Cader Idris.

through the Dulas and Corris valleys to Dolgelley. Situated in the valley of the Dovey, a famous fishing river, it can lay strong claims, for historic events have taken place within its borders. It was at Machynlleth that Owen Glyndwr held a Parliament in 1402, and the house in which it was held is now restored and forms the Owen Glyndwr Institute. After crossing the River Dovey the train passes through Ffridd-Wood and enters upon a scene of great beauty, which is said to bear exact resemblance to the Royal Drive at Balmoral. Foliage of every description meets the eye of the traveller.

A number of waterfalls and millstreams are next seen and a most enchanting bit of river fringed with trees, and further on a natural canal of considerable length, where the river has cut its way through the rock.

Esgairgeiliog is then reached, close to which is an exceedingly pretty bridge, and just beyond the miniature Horse Shoe Falls, where there is a charming spectacle of the river dashing over a natural rocky weir, falling in cascades and then running in rocky gorges. The next station is Corris, where the traveller to Talyllyn Lake or Cader Idris changes for the motor coach stage of the journey.

Many pretty walks there are, however, around Corris, and the disciple of Izaak Walton can have very fair sport ; salmon, sewin and trout being found in the Dulas, which is free from Corris to its source.

Photo—Culliford.

Plascrug Avenue.

From Corris through the summer months, the trip to Talyllyn Lake can be made in the luxurious motor coaches of the Corris Railway Company. This daily service in connection with the Great Western Railway affords splendid facilities to the visitor from Aberystwyth, who can obtain a combined rail and motor ticket at his starting point, and can leave Aberystwyth in the morning, arrive at the foot of Cader Idris without walking, have four or five hours on the mountain, or boating or fishing on Talyllyn Lake, and yet be enabled to return home in the early evening.

Talyllyn Lake, at the foot of the mountain, presents a charming spectacle. It is one of the prettiest lakes in Wales, and every day in the summer swarms of visitors picnic by its beautiful shore. For this purpose it is an ideal spot ; fishing, climbing or exploring can be indulged in to the full, and what more enjoyable or health giving, in such delightful surroundings ! Talyllyn Church, close to the lake, is well worth a visit. It is early English, and is believed to date from the sixth or seventh century.

*Photo—Culliford*

North Parade, Aberystwyth.

*Photo—Culliford.*

Children's Lake.   Fleet in the background.

## ROYAL PATRONAGE.

KING EDWARD, then Prince of Wales, visited the town in 1896, on the occasion of his installation as Chancellor of the University. Before leaving the town the Prince telegraphed to Queen Victoria :—" I am delighted with this pretty place, and the perfect way everything has been arranged." The occasion was also memorable by the fact that it was Mr.Gladstone's last public appearance, the eminent statesmen travelling from Hawarden to accept an honorary degree ; and the Princess of Wales (now Queen Alexandra) received the degree of Doctor of Music and formally opened the Alexandra Hall of Residence for Women Students. This ancient borough has on several occasions since been honoured by members of the Royal Family, the Prince of Wales making a visit as recently as October 1923. The King, accompanied by the Queen, Prince of Wales and Princess Mary laid the foundation stone of the National Library in 1912.

## THE UNIVERSITY COLLEGE OF WALES.

NEAR the ruins of its ancient Castle, the University College of Wales, founded by patriotic effort in 1872, towers aloft facing the sea, the first Constituent College of the University of Wales of which the King is Protector and the Prince of Wales its Chancellor. Its growth has been phenomenal, and its success a veritable romance. To cope with its growing work, additional institutions became necessary—the Chemistry Laboratory on Buarth, the Agricultural Laboratory, the Music House, the College Hall in North Road, etc.—and there are no better hostels for women students to be found in any place than the Alexandra Hall and Carpenter Hall on the Terrace. After the war, there were over 1,100 students in residence—in Arts, Science, Law, Music, Agriculture—students drawn from every portion of the Principality and other countries, who are trained for their degrees in the Welsh University at a reasonable cost well within the means of the working peasant. The old students occupy some of the highest positions in the academic world, and they regularly revisit the town during the re-union week at Easter, for whom the " Union," newly built, will be a great boon. Among the most recent extensions of the teaching activity of the College one can mention the establishment of the National School of Music, the foundation of the Chair of International Politics, the institution of the Plant Breeding Station—all due to the generosity of benevolent benefactors. The College Model Farm, one of the best in the County, is on the other side of the Vale of Clarach—an easy and interesting walk from the town. The students, 900 in number, are in residence from October to June, and are away on holiday while the visitors in their thousands arrive for the summer months.

*Photo—Culliford.*

Rocks under Constitution Hill.

*Photo—Culliford.*

Portion of Castle Grounds and War Memorial.

# MUSICAL FACILITIES.

As a result of the report of a Royal Commission on University education in Wales, the National Council of Music was formed, and the acceptance by Sir Walford Davies in 1919 of the important dual posts of Director of Music for the University and Professor of Music at Aberystwyth College was the marking of a new era in the musical life of the principality. Since the advent of the National Council of Music the aim and policy have been to concentrate not so much on the granting of degrees as upon the making of music a vital factor in University life. In this policy the Council of Music include the permanent institution of weekly College Concerts ; College Choral and Orchestral Unions ; Open Lectures weekly in Music. Special facilities are also offered to Students who are becoming teachers in Schools to learn an instrument. A feature of College Musical life at Aberystwyth has been the annual three days' Orchestral Festival.

Degrees and diplomas in Music are granted at Aberystwyth College—residence is required for both, and an efficient staff is appointed to provide tuition in the various branches of musical education.

## THE NATIONAL LIBRARY OF WALES,

THE Library is maintained by an annual grant from the Treasury. The object for which the Library was founded is to collect, preserve and make available for use by research workers and others, all books, manuscripts, documents, and all other literary and scientific works in Welsh or any other Celtic language, or which deal with the Welsh and other Celtic peoples ; and further works on all subjects and in all languages which help to attain the purposes for which the University of Wales, the University Colleges, schools and other educational institutions in Wales were founded.

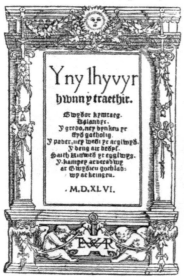

First Book printed in Welsh, 1546.

The collection of Welsh printed books and manuscripts, the most valuable portion of which is due to the munificence of its President, Sir John Williams, Bart., G.C.V.O., is the finest in the world. He had purchased the Welsh portion of the library of the Earl of Macclesfield,

Shirburn Castle (Oxfordshire), and the manuscripts from the Peniarth Library (Merioneth), which, together with his own collection of Welsh books and manuscripts, he presented to the Library on the 1st January, 1909. Other well-known collections acquired at the same time or subsequently,

Waterfalls, Devil's Bridge.

by gift, purchase, bequest or on deposit, include the Mostyn, Dingestow Court, Panton, "Gwallter Mechain," Kinmel and Llan-over Manuscripts, and the Wynn-Gwydir, Panton, and Williams-Wynn papers and correspondence. Included in these or other collections are *The Black Book of Carmarthen*, the oldest manuscript in the Welsh language, written at Carmarthen at the end of the twelfth century; many of the oldest manuscripts of Welsh poetry, for example, the Gogynfoirdd MSS. containing poems of the bards of the periods of the independent Welsh princes; the oldest manuscripts of the Mabinogion, the Welsh laws, and the Bruts or Chronicles. The Library has also a valuable manuscript of Chaucer's *Canterbury Tales* (The Hengwrt Chaucer).

Since July 1912, the Library, under the Copyright Act of 1911, has been entitled to claim a copy of all books, pamphlets, maps, volume and sheet-music, etc., published within the British

Exhibition Gallery, National Library.

Isles, a privilege it enjoys in common with five other principal libraries in Great Britain and Ireland. This alone meant growth at the rate of about 35,000 items annually, and has assisted materially towards realising the second purpose defined by the charter, namely the formation of a general reference library, where students and workers may obtain material for their work. The Library has also, by purchase, gift or bequest, made notable accessions in general literature. For example, it has a superb collection of early French romances, printed and manuscript; its collection of early editions and manuscripts of *Le Roman de la Rose* is among the finest in the world.

The number of printed volumes approaches half-a-million, of manuscripts 6,000, whilst deeds, documents and records generally number about 50,000. There is also a large collection of maps, portraits, topographical prints and drawings dealing with Wales and the four border counties. By the installation of the photostat, the gift of Major Lewis J. Mathias, C.B.E., D.L., of Aberystwyth, the Library is able to supply facsimile copies of books, manuscripts and documents of all kinds for the use of research workers who are unable to visit Aberystwyth. The Library is available for use, without charge, by any responsible person who obtains a ticket of admission as a reader, for which

South Wing of the National Library of Wales.

forms of application are obtainable at the Library. The Library Hall Readers Room is open to readers daily from 10 to 5, except on Bank Holidays, and at such other times as the Council may determine.

For visitors and the general public an Exhibition, representative of the contents of the various departments, has been arranged in the Exhibition Gallery, open free 10 to 5 daily (except Sundays) from May to September, and at other times on application. In the Exhibition Gallery are arranged manuscripts, rare and beautiful books (including books in fine bindings), portraits of Welsh celebrities and personalia relating to them, autograph letters, paintings (on loan from the Tate Gallery, London, and other sources). A general catalogue of the contents of the exhibition, with notes on the artists represented by paintings, is on sale at the Library. An extensive series of pictorial postcards, giving views of the buildings and reproductions of some of the paintings, books and manuscripts exhibited, is also on sale.

## PUBLICATIONS.

A card catalogue of printed books is in course of preparation and can be consulted in the Catalogue Room, at the entrance to the Library Hall. In addition, several catalogues of special subjects, and of exhibitions arranged from time to time have been issued : Bibliotheca Celtica, a register of publications relating to Wales and the Celtic peoples and languages for the years 1909-18 ; Catalogue of Tracts of the Civil War and the Commonwealth period relating to Wales and the borders, Aberystwyth, 1911 ; a Bibliography of Robert Owen, the Socialist, Aberystwyth, 1914.

Principal Administrative Officers :—Librarian, John Ballinger, C.B.E., M.A. ; Assistant Librarian, William Ll. Davies, M.A. ; Secretary to the Librarian, D. Julian Jones.

## PLACES OF WORSHIP.
### ENGLISH.

**St. Michael's Church.** *Vicar* : CANON D. WILLIAMS.
**Holy Trinity Church.** *Vicar* : THE VEN. ARCHDEACON WILLIAMS.
**Roman Catholic.** REV. FATHER PAUL HOOK.
**Congregational Church, Portland Street.** *Resident Minister* : REV. G. BENTON.
**Wesley Church, Queen's Road.** *Resident Minister* : REV. I. A. CLAPPERTON.
**Presbyterian Church, Bath Street.** REV. R. HUGHES.
**Baptist Church, Alfred Place.** REV. J. W. HUGHES.
**New Street Meeting House.** MR. EYRE EVANS.

### WELSH.

**St. Mary's Church, Gray's Inn Road.** CANON D. WILLIAMS.
**Calvinistic Methodist Chapels.**
　　**Tabernacle, Powell Street.** REV. J. D. EVANS.
　　**Shiloh, North Parade.** REV. T. E. ROBERTS.
　　**Salem, Portland Street.** REV. J. DAVIES.
**Wesleyan Methodist Chapels.**
　　**St. Paul's, Great Darkgate Street,** and **Siloam, Cambrian Street.** REV. EVAN ISAAC.
**Baptist Chapel, Baker Street.** REV. JOS. EDWARDS.
**Independent Chapel, Baker Street.** REV. PETER PRICE.
**Church Army, Trefechan.** CAPT. MORRIS.
**Salvation Army, Railway Terrace.**

North Beach, as seen from Royal Pier.

Hafod, where Handel composed the Hallelujah Chorus.

# ABERYSTWYTH—A SPORTSMAN'S MECCA.

## Golf, Tennis, Bowls, Croquet, and Fishing and Boating.

ONE of the many advantages possessed by Aberystwyth is the accessibility of its facilities for sport. All the playing fields are within easy walking distance from any part of the town.

**Golf.**—The eighteen-hole Golf Course is on Bryn-y-Mor, north-east of the town, amid beautiful undulating upland country. It was planned by Harry Vardon, and presents a large variety of hazards, and is excellently situated quite near the Promenade, commanding an excellent view of the Bay. The qualifying round of the *Daily Mail* £1,000 Tournament (Welsh Section) was played on this course in April 1923. The professional record, which is held by James Braid and by W. C. Ireland, a former professional coach to the Club, is 68, while the amateur record of 70 is held by Prof. Ed. Edwards, M.A., Vice-Principal of the U.C.W., Aberystwyth. Daily, weekly, fortnightly and monthly tickets may be obtained by visitors at the commodious club-house.

**Tennis.**—Eleven first-class hard tennis courts, laid by the " En Tout Cas Co.," were opened Easter, 1923. There is a fine pavilion, including a large tea-room and ladies' and gentlemen's rooms, with shower baths. The main entrance is from Queen's Road. Daily, weekly and monthly tickets are issued to visitors.

Thirteen grass courts in the U.C.W. Athletic Grounds, Llanbadarn Road, are available for play during July, August and September.

**Bowls.**—The two full-sized bowling greens, beautifully situated in Plascrug, near the railway station, are open to visitors, and daily, weekly, monthly and season tickets are issued.

**Croquet, etc.,** may be played in the U.C.W. Athletic Grounds on application being made to the groundsman.

**Fishing.**—The fresh-water fishermen will find good trout fishing in the neighbourhood. Sir Lewes Loveden Pryse, Bart., has opened his waters to the public at very moderate charges. 5s. and 10s. season tickets may be obtained.

The Angling Association have four strictly preserved lakes, and a limited number of members is accepted. A limited number of day tickets may be obtained. The various streams of the neighbourhood afford many other facilities. For further particulars, apply to the Secretary.

There is excellent sea-fishing all the year round. (See separate article.)

**Boating** is provided by boats of all sizes, which are annually inspected and licensed by the Corporation. A number of motor launches also ply daily on the beach and make trips around the coast.

En Tout Cas Tennis Courts, Aberystwyth.

BRITISH
PUBLISHING
COMPANY

# SEA FISHING.

IN addition to the many facilities for river and lake fishing exist-
ent in the neighbourhood, sea-fishing, which can be done with
fly as well as with ground bait, affords equally good sport, and,
in addition, has the advantages of being open all the year round
and free from the restrictions of Boards of Conservators, riparian
owners, and water bailiffs. Cardigan Bay is the feeding ground
for fish of the Atlantic. Great gutters run from New Quay Head
towards Aberystwyth in which local and other trawlers reap
rich harvests of sole, turbot, brill and plaice. Ambitious fishermen
may do worse than make a cruise in a trawler on one of its visits
to the grounds. Line-fishing from a boat, from the reefs, from
the new Promenade, or from the stone pier at the Harbour, will,
however, be more suitable for the majority ; and bass, whiting
pollack, mackerel, whiting, and mullet fishing is not by any
means to be despised. Bass is as sporting a fish as a
salmon. They appear in the bay about May, and remain till
July, and can be taken with the Alexander fly or by ground bait.
Mackerel, with which the sea sometimes teems, run from May till
August, mullet from June to September, gurnet from May to
August, and whiting from September to March.

## PLACES OF INTEREST NEAR ABERYSTWYTH.

MANY places of
exceptional
interest and
beauty in the neighbour-
hood make Aberystwyth
a splendid jumping-off
place for both visitors
and residents.

As a glance at the
map will show, the
geographical situation of
Aberystwyth is practic-
ally in the centre of the
coast-line forming Cardi-
gan Bay, thus giving it
a unique position as the
best starting-place to
any part of Wales.

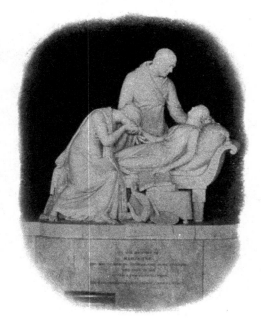

Chantrey's masterpiece in marble, in
the church of Eglwys Newydd, Hafod.

1. Pontrhydygroes.
2. Llanbadarn Cathedral Church.
3. Penybont Bridge and Pen Dinas.

As before stated the environs of Aberystwyth are peculiarly beautiful, scarcely any part of the Kingdom being so favourably situated. Whether along the vales of the River Rheidol, or the Ystwyth, or on the mountains : whether the prospective visitor be pedestrian, cyclist or motorist : whether antiquary, naturalist, sportsman, or fisherman, every taste is served : the different features of the landscape vieing with each other in presenting all those changes that charm and serve for recreation.

Charming rural walks are available, and the fauna and flora of river, wood, heath and fields, are extraordinarily rich in variety. A list of adjacent places of interest is appended, and it is only to be regretted that the space at our disposal will not allow us to dilate upon the exceptional features peculiar to each.

**Devil's Bridge and the Falls.** Wonderful sight. Unrivalled in grandeur.

**Parsons Bridge,** near Devil's Bridge. Remarkable scenery.

**Hafod and Hafod Church.** Chantrey's masterpiece, and most gorgeous scenery around.

**Pontrhydygroes and the Ystwyth Valley.** Very charming.

**Crosswood Park** (Earl Lisburne). Lovely drive.

**Strataflorida Abbey.** Well worth seeing—described as the Westminster of Wales.

**Talybont.** Pretty village. Taliesin Grave, not far.

**Corris Railway and Machynlleth.** Magnificent scenery on to Corris, etc.

**Talyllyn Lake.** Very beautiful, at the foot of Cader.

**Llyfnant Valley.** One of the best valleys in Wales, and picture of loveliness.

**Nanteos.** A short distance, and beautifully situated, contains the Tregaron Healing Cup, which resembles the Holy Grail.

**Gogerddan Park.** The seat of Sir Lewes Loveden Pryse.

**Llanbadarn Cathedral Church.** Founded by St. Padarn, contains the grave of Lewis Morris, the Welsh poet.

**Clarach Valley, Llangorwen Church, Cwm Mansion,** where John Keble wrote most of his well-known *Christian Year,* and the birth-place of Isaac Williams, the poet and hymnist.

**Monk's Cave.** Known also as Twll-Twrw and the Thunder Hole.

**Rheidol Falls.** One of the finest afternoon drives.

## BY MOTOR CHAR-A-BANC FROM ABERYSTWYTH.
### Full Day.

Llandrindod Wells, via Plymlymon, Llangurig, Rhayader and Wye Valley. Wonderful and romantic drive.

Dolgelley, via Cader Idris Pass, Dolgelley, Fairbourne Towyn and Aberdorey. Magnificent drive.

Birmingham Water Works and Elan Valley, via Graiggoch and Caregddu Dams ; going through some beautiful scenery.

Glaspwll, Llyfnant Valley.

Talyllyn Lake, via Eglwysfach, Corris, Foot of Cader Idris, and
   return via Towyn and Aberdorey.

New Quay, via Llanrhystid, Aberarth, Llanarth and Aberayron.

Circular Tour, via Llanidloes, Llandinain and Cemmes Road.

Dinas Mawddwy, via Machyulleth, Cemmes and Mallwyd.

Lampeter, via Strataflorida, returning via Aberayron.

Hafod Church, via Devil's Bridge, Hafod Grounds, Pontrhydygroes, Crosswood and Llanilar.

Llyfnant Valley, via Bow Street and Glandovey.

Cardigan, via Tresaith and Llangranog.  Lovely spots.

## Half-day or Afternoon Drives.

Devil's Bridge, via Penparke and return via Parsons Bridge and
   Ponterwyd.

New Panorama—Borth, via Ynyslas, Taliesin, Talybont and
   Gogerddan, Loves Grove and Llanbadarn.

Panorama—Nanteos, Crosswood and Llanilar.

Aberayron, all on the sea coast.

Rheidol Falls, via Llanbadarn and Capel Bangor.

## TABLE OF DISTANCES.

| Walks. | miles. | | miles. |
|---|---|---|---|
| Ropewalk Hill | 0 | Borth | 7 |
| Plas Crug Avenue | 0 | Ynyslas | 10 |
| Elysian Grove | 0 | Craigypistyll | 8½ |
| Penybont Bridge | 1 | Panorama Drive | 8 |
| Penparke | 1 | Capel Bangor | 5 |
| Llanbadarn Church | 1 | Monks' Caves | 5 |
| Constitution Hill | 0¼ | Rheidol Falls | 9 |
| Pen Dinas | 1 | Talybont | 7½ |
| Brynymor | 0½ | Devil's Bridge | 12 |
| Penglaise Hill | 1 | Glandovey | 15 |
| Alltwen Cliffs | 1½ | Llanrhystyd | 9 |
| Blackberry Lane | 1 | Llyfnant Valley | 16 |
| Clarach Beach | 1½ | Artists' Valley | 16 |
| Cwm Woods | 1½ | Taliesin's Grave | 10 |
| Llangorwen Church | 2 | | |
| Llanychaiarn Church | 2½ | **Excursions.** | |
| Nanteos | 3 | Strata Florida | 15 |
| Wallog Reefs | 3 | Devil's Bridge Drive | 12 |
| Gogerddan | 3½ | Plimlymon Mountain | 16 |
| | | Pontrhydygroes | 15 |
| **Outings.** | | Hafod | 17 |
| Llanilar | 6 | Cader Idris Mountain | 26 |
| Pontrhydybeddau | 7 | Teify Pools | 19 |
| Melindwr Valley | 6 | Aberayron | 16 |

82

Rheidol Valley, Aberystwyth.

Ystwyth Valley.

## PUBLIC AND OTHER BUILDINGS.

Town Hall,
University College,
National Library of Wales,
Public Library,
Carnegie Library,

Royal Pavilion,

Parish Hall,
Coliseum,
College Hall,
Assembly Rooms (Old Georgian
  Building where Sir Henry Irving
  played *The Bells* for the first time.
College Memorial Hall, as Club.

### CLUBS.

St. David's Club ... ... ... Pier Street
Conservative Club ... ... ... Little Darkgate Street
National Liberal Club ... ... Market Square
Independent Liberal Club ... ... North Parade
The Y.M.C.A. Memorial Hall ... Chalybeate Street
The Y.W.C.A. ... ... ... North Parade and Queen's Square

### PLACES OF AMUSEMENT, CONCERTS, &c.

Municipal Band on the Parade
Castle Grounds Pavilion
Royal Pier Pavilion ... ... Seat about 2,000
The Cinema ... ... ... ... Market Street
The College Central Hall, ... ... Seat over 3,000. Queen's Road and
  London Symphony Orchestra        North Road
The Parish Hall ... ... ... St. Michael's Place
The Coliseum ... ... ... Terrace Road. Seat about 2,000
The Imperial Cinema ... ... Bath Street
The Quarryettes ... ... ... Queen's Road
The Elysian Grove ... ... ... Penglais Road

### NEWSPAPERS.

Cambrian News ... ... ... Published on Thursday
Welsh Gazette ... ... ... Published on Wednesday

*Photo by Major Matthews.*

Aberystwyth Golf Club House.

84

# Apartments and Boarding Houses.

**MRS. ROWLAND,**
Oxford House, 4 MARINE TERRACE.
Private, Superior Apartments.
Near Golf, Tennis Courts and
Bowling Green.
Highly recommended.

**MRS. LLEW ROWLANDS,**
Welwyn House,
No. 6 MARINE TERRACE.
Private Apartments.
3 Sitting Rooms.     10 Bedrooms.
Close to Pier and Band, also Golf,
Tennis and Bowling.  Recommended.

**MRS. MASSEY,**
14 MARINE TERRACE,
(facing Sea)
Private Apartments or Board.
3 Sitting Rooms.     10 Bedrooms.

**MISS EVANS,**
Cambridge House,
15 MARINE TERRACE.
Private Apartments.
3 Sitting Rooms.     15 Bedrooms.
Near Golf, Tennis Courts & Bowling.

**MRS. JONES,**
Garfield House,
16 MARINE TERRACE.
Private Apartments.
2 Sitting Rooms.     8 Bedrooms.
Very central. Near Golf, Tennis
Courts and Bowling.

**MISS NEALE & MRS. ROWLANDS,**
18 MARINE TERRACE.
Boarding House.
4 Sitting Rooms.     14 Bedrooms.
Bath, h. & c.  Central.  Moderate
charges. Near Golf, Tennis Courts
and Bowling.

**MRS. POTTS,**
19 MARINE TERRACE.
Private Apartments or Board.
Modern Conveniences and Superior.

**MRS. VAUGHAN,**
20 MARINE TERRACE.
Private Superior Apartments.
Close to Pier and Band.
Near Golf, Tennis Courts & Bowling.
Central.

**MRS. PHILP,**
Belgrave, 24 MARINE TERRACE.
Board and Private Apartments.
4 Sitting Rooms.     12 Bedrooms.
Nicely situated.
Near Golf, Tennis Courts & Bowling.
Moderate Charges.

**MRS. HUGHES,**
Brynymor, 35 MARINE TERRACE.
Board and Private Apartments.
4 Sitting Rooms.     12 Bedrooms.
Highly recommended.
Close to Golf, Tennis Cts. & Bowling.

**MRS. JAMES,**
Moreland House,
36 MARINE TERRACE.
Private Apartments.
4 Sitting Rooms.     14 Bedrooms.
Good Cooking and Attendance.
Near Golf, Tennis Courts & Bowling.

**MRS. GRAHAM,**
37 MARINE TERRACE.
Private and Board Residence.
3 Sitting Rooms.     10 Bedrooms.
Liberal Table.   Finest position on
front and Band Stand.

**MISS BIDDULPH,**
Caradoc House,
38 MARINE TERRACE.
3 Private Sitting Rooms. 7 Bedrooms.
Central position.
Near Golf, Tennis Courts & Bowling.

**MISS DAVIES,**
Picton House,
43 MARINE TERRACE,
(facing Sea)
Private and Boarding.
Near Golf, Tennis and Bowls.

**MRS. C. J. LONG,**
45 THE TERRACE.
Private Apartments and Boarding.
3 Sitting Rooms.     7 Bedrooms.
Bath, h. & c. Nicely situated. Close
to Band, near Golf, Tennis Courts and
Bowling.

**MRS. J. C. MORGAN,**
Glandulas, 47 MARINE TERRACE.
Private Apartments.
4 Sitting Rooms.     11 Bedrooms.
Good position.
Close to Tennis, Links and Bowling.

**MR. G. F. WEBB,**
Wolverhampton House,
53 MARINE TERRACE.
Private and Boarding.
3 Sitting Rooms.     12 Bedrooms.
Near Golf, Tennis Courts & Bowling.

**MRS. KIRKHAM,** (Late Birmingham)
Penbryn House,
55 MARINE TERRACE.
Boarding Establishment.
4 Sitting Rooms.     12 Bedrooms.
Near Golf, Tennis Cts. & Bowling.

**MRS. SUTHERLAND,**
Clive House,
56 MARINE TERRACE.
Board and Private Apartments.
4 Sitting Rooms.     12 Bedrooms.
Full view of Bay.   Home comforts.

**MRS. G. B. FARROW,**
East Langdon,
57 MARINE TERRACE.
Good position.   Board Residence.
Close to Links,  Tennis and Bowling.

# Apartments and Boarding Houses.

**MISSES DUGGAN,**
Idris House,
58 MARINE TERRACE.
Private Apartments.
3 Sitting Rooms.    7 Bedrooms.
Pleasant situation.
Close to Bathing Beach. Central.

**MRS. PATERSON,**
Oban House, 60 MARINE TERRACE.
Private Apartments.
3 Sitting Rooms.    8 Bedrooms.
Bath, h. & c.   Good Cooking and
Attention.   Near Golf, Tennis and
Bowling.

**HAWKETTS,**
The Rivals, 61 MARINE TERRACE.
Private Apartments.
3 Sitting Rooms.    7 Bedrooms.
Bath, h. & c.   Very comfortable
Near Links, Tennis, &c.

**MISS PRICE,**
62 MARINE TERRACE.
Boarding.
3 Sitting Rooms.    7 Bedrooms.
▸▾ Best part of the Promenade.
Near Golf, Tennis and Bowling.

**MRS. JAMES,**
St. Davids,
63 MARINE TERRACE.
Private Apartments.
4 Sitting Rooms.    12 Bedrooms.
Moderate.   Near Links, Tennis and
Bowling.   Comfortable.

**MISS E. NELSON,**
York House,
64 MARINE TERRACE.
Private Apartments.
4 Sitting Rooms.    10 Bedrooms.
Near Links, Tennis and Bowling.

**MRS. JONES,**
Clifton House,
65 MARINE TERRACE.
Private Apartments.
3 Sitting Rooms.    10 Bedrooms.
Near Links, Tennis and Bowling.
Moderate.

**MISSES COCKBILL,**
St. Anthony,
VICTORIA TERRACE
(facing Sea)
Boarding Establishment.
Excellent situation.   Near Golf,
Tennis and Bowls.

**MISS MASSEY,**
Craiglais, VICTORIA TERRACE.
(Detached House)
Private and Boarding.
5 Sitting Rooms.    10 Bedrooms.
Electric Light.   Excellent situation.
Near  Golf,  Tennis  and  Bowling.

**MISS KNIGHT,**
Glanydon, 5 SOUTH MARINE TERRACE.
Private Apartments.
(facing Sea)
3  Sitting  Rooms.    7  Bedrooms.
Close to Church and Castle.
Good Cooking.        Recommended.

**MRS. SPELLER,**
Forteviot,
6 SOUTH MARINE TER.
Private Apartments.
2  Sitting  Rooms.    7  Bedrooms.
Nicely situated, and near Castle G'ds.

**PROPRIETRESS,**
7  SOUTH  MARINE  TERRACE.
Boarding House
Beautiful Situation and Outlook.
Near Castle.   Recommended.

**MRS. EDWARDS,**
Morawel, 9 SOUTH MARINE TERRACE.
Private Apartments.
3 Sitting Rooms.    7 Bedrooms.
Bath, h. & c.   Excellent   situation.
Near Castle Grounds.

**MISS THOMAS,**
Brynarfor, 12 SOUTH MARINE TER.
Private Apartments.
3 Sitting Rooms.    7 Bedrooms.
Bath, h. & c.        Good situation.
Near Castle Grounds.

**MRS. W. J. PUGH,**
14 SOUTH MARINE TERRACE.
Furnished House to Let, July,
August and September.
Apply early.
3 Sitting Rooms.    8 Bedrooms.
Plate and Linen supplied.

**MRS. PALMER,**
No. 15 SOUTH MARINE TERRACE.
Private Apartments.
2 Sitting Rooms.    7 Bedrooms.
Sea  front.   Bathing  from  House.

**MRS. EVANS,**
Bengair, 17 SOUTH MARINE TERRACE.
Superior Private Apartments.
Best position.
Good Cooking and Attendance.
Highly recommended,

**MRS T. WILLIAMS,**
Eastnor, 18 SOUTH MARINE TER.
Private Apartments.
3 Sitting Rooms.    6 Bedrooms.
Electric Light.   Facing sea.   Bathing
from house.   Good Cooking.

**MRS. EDWARDS,**
Gwenydon, CLIFF TERRACE.
Boarding Establishment.
Bath,   h. & c.   Excellent   position.
Facing Sea.   Close to Golf, Tennis
and Bowling.
Electric Light throughout.

**MRS. MARSH,**
Aelydon, CLIFF TERRACE.
Private Apartments.
1 Sitting Room.    4 Bedrooms.
Bath, h. & c.   Electric Light.   Facing
sea.   Lovely situation.
Close to Golf, Tennis and Bowling.

# Apartments and Boarding Houses.

**MISS SMITH,**
Aventine, CLIFF TERRACE.
Boarding Establishment.
Good position. Close to front,
Golf, Tennis and Bowling.
Bath, h. & c.

**MRS. THOMAS,**
Dumbarton,
ALBERT PLACE
(facing Queen's Hotel entrance).
Private Apartments.
2 Sitting Rooms and 6 Bedrooms.
Near Golf and Tennis Courts.

**MRS. BULLOCK,**
Landmarsh House.
QUEEN'S ROAD.
Private Apartments.
2 Sitting Rooms. 6 Bedrooms.
Central for all parts. Good Cooking.

**MRS. SHEWRING,**
Aubbrey House,
QUEEN'S ROAD,
Private and Board Residence.
3 Sitting Rooms. 9 Bedrooms.
Very central. Good Cooking and
attendance. Terms Moderate.

**MISS JENKINS,**
Belair, QUEEN'S ROAD.
Private Apartments.
3 Sitting Rooms. 10 Bedrooms.
Highly recommended. Close to sea,
Golf, Tennis and Bowling.

**MISS BELL,**
Westdene, QUEEN'S ROAD,
(Cambridge Terrace).
Private Apartments.
3 Sitting Rooms. 8 Bedrooms.
Bath, h. & c. Close to sea, Golf,
Tennis and Bowling.

**MRS. J. L. JONES,**
Meirionfa, QUEEN'S ROAD.
Private and Boarding Apartments.
4 Sitting Rooms. 11 Bedrooms.
Bath, h. & c. Home comforts. Close
to sea, Golf, Tennis and Bowling.

**MRS. LEWIS,**
Crystal Palace Hotel,
QUEEN'S ROAD.
Private Apartments or Board.
Refurnished and re-decorated.
Pleasant situation and Central. New
Proprietorship.

**MRS. R. W. WILLIAMS,**
" Roseville,"
Cambridge Terrace,
QUEEN'S ROAD.
Private Apartments.
2 Sitting Rooms. 8 Bedrooms.
Highly recommended, close to Sea,
Golf, Tennis and Bowling.

**MRS. NORTHWOOD,**
Cefn Hendre Farm, LLANBADARN.
(1¼ miles from Town)
Private and Boarding.
2 Sitting Rooms and 5 Bedrooms.
Recommended. Piano.
Motor 'Bus passing daily.

**J. MARTIN,**
Prince Albert Hotel,
LITTLE DARKGATE ST.
Bath, h. & c. One minute from front.
With or without Board.
Excellent Accommodation. Garage.
Moderate Terms.

**MRS. DAVIES,**
Glenelva,
32 ALEXANDRA ROAD.
Private Apartments.
2 Sitting Rooms. 6 Bedrooms.
Close to Sea and Station.
Also Plascrug Avenue, To Let.

**MRS. PRICE,**
Bryn-Al-Ban,
NORTH ROAD.
Superior and Modern Residence,
beautifully situated. Close to Prom-
enade, Golf, Tennis and Bowls.
To let July and August.
2 Sitting Rooms and 5 Bedrooms.
Please apply early.

**MRS. ARTHUR M. GODWIN,**
(Late of Selly Oak, Birmingham)
" Eastwood,"
ELM TREE AVENUE,
Plascrug.
Private Apartments.
Near Station and Sea. All Modern
Improvements. Central for Golf,
Bowls and Tennis.
Telegraphic Address :
" Godwin, Eastwood, Aberystwyth."

**MRS. HUGHES,** Reliance House, CASTLE STREET (Close to Castle Entrance).
Apartments and Board. Recommended.

# University College
# of Wales, Aberystwyth

PRESIDENT:

**SIR JOHN WILLIAMS, Bart., M.D., D.Sc., G.C.V.O.**

PRINCIPAL:

**JOHN HUMPHREYS DAVIES, M.A. (Oxon.)**

THE SESSION begins in September. Lectures commence early in October. Entrance Scholarships and Exhibitions, open to both male and female candidates above the age of sixteen, are offered for competition at the commencement of the Session. Students are prepared for Degrees in Arts, Science (including the Applied Science of Agriculture), Law and Music. Men Students reside in registered lodgings in the town, or at the Men's Hostel. Women Students reside in the Hall of Residence for Women. For full particulars respecting Fees, etc., apply to:—

THE GENERAL SECRETARY.

One of the latest additions to the Buildings is a **College Hall** (situated in **North Road**) capable of accommodating **3,000** people. The College is prepared to let the Hall on reasonable terms for large Concerts, Musical Festivals, Eisteddfodau, etc.

Aberystwyth's Mountainous Hinterland.

# Start SPRING CLEANING Early

# ABERYSTWYTH
# GOLF LINKS

Splendid 18-Hole Course. Over-looking Town and Bay. Magnificent Sea and Mountain Views.

Professional  -  A. BENNETT.

New Club House, Visitors cordially welcomed. First Tee, 15 minutes from Promenade. "Daily Mail" Competition (Qualifying Round), Welsh Section, 18th April, 1923

---

*The Green Fees are as follows :—*

Daily : Ladies, 2/6 ; Gents, 3/6
Monthly :    do.    £1 ;    do.    £1-10-0

| Weekly : | 1st July to 30th Sept. | | 1st Oct. to 30th June |
|---|---|---|---|
| Ladies | ..... | 10/- | ..... | 6/- |
| Gents | ..... | 12/6 | ..... | 7/6 |
| Fortnightly : | | | |
| Ladies | ..... | 15/- | ..... | 8/- |
| Gents | ..... | £1 | ...... | 10/6 |

Boys and Girls under 17 years of age :—
Day, 2/6 ;  Week, 7/6 ;  Fortnight, 12/- ;  Month, 15/-.
Country Membership.

---

*For further particulars apply to :—*

# G. B. FARROW, Secretary,
57 Marine Terrace, or
# Councillor T. H. EDWARDS, Hon. Sec.,
### ABERYSTWYTH

92

# St. Padarn's Convent School for Girls

## BOARDING AND DAY SCHOOL

Healthy and picturesque situation. Pupils prepared for University Locals, Associated Board of Music and Royal Drawing Society Examinations.

FURTHER PARTICULARS ON APPLICATION TO THE REV. MOTHER

St. Padarn's Convent, Aberystwyth.

# ROBERTS

## Family Butchers

102

# D. LLOYD, Grocer & Provision Merchant

**North End Stores, Alexandra Road, ABERYSTWYTH**

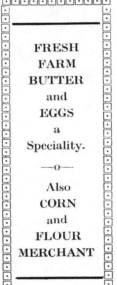

# The Market Street Cinema

"THE HOUSE OF DISTINCTION"

The FIRST Picture House in Aberystwyth (Established 1910)
Altered, Re-seated and Re-organised in 1923

The Last Word in Comfort and Beauty :—Perfect Ventilation,
Faultless Projection, Brilliant Music, High-Class Programmes

## DISTINCTIVE IN EVERY SENSE OF THE WORD

For Times of Showing, etc., see Daybills

# D. JONES & SONS

## FAMILY BUTCHERS

*Welsh Mutton and Lamb a Speciality*

# The Central Meat Stores

## 5 NORTH PARADE AND
## 3 NORTH GATE STREET
## —— ABERYSTWYTH ——

# H. J. EDWARDS

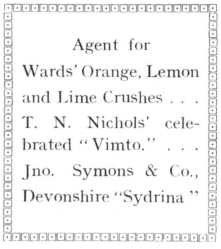

# Baker St., Aberystwyth

SOLE AGENT :—
Nobel's Explosives Co. Ltd.
Walter A. Wood Mower Co.
"Devon" Fires.

Ranges, Grates, Builders'
Ironmongery, Farming
Implements, Quarry &
Mining Requisites,
Explosives and
Cartridges

**A. W. VIGARS** (T. L. OLD)

LAMPS

Enamelled and
Aluminium
Household Goods.

Joiners'
and Farmers' Tools.

"Valor-Perfection" and
"B.P." Oil Cooking Stoves.

"TRIPLEX"
COMBINATION GRATES

"HERALD" and
"GRADIENT" RANGES

117

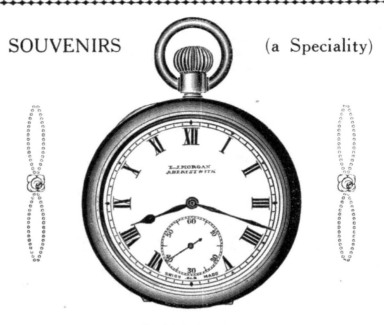

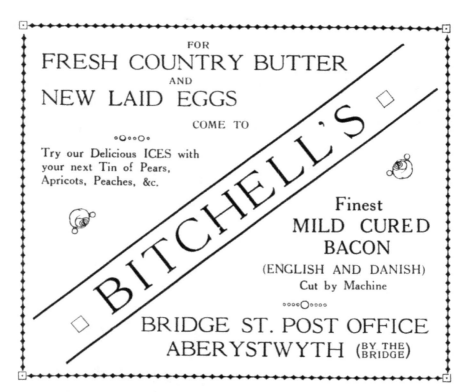

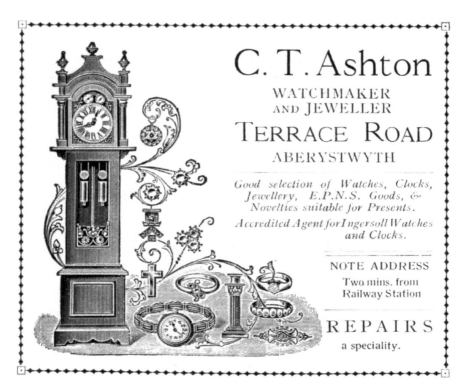

126

G T BASSETT. A RIBA
ARCHITECT

R & H L OWEN
BUILDERS & CONTRACTORS
36ᴬ QUEEN STREET
ABERYSTWYTH

134

# HOWELL & CO.

A Firm with a reputation of nearly a century.

Leaders of fashion in 'all goods appertaining to Ladies' and Gent's Wear.

Specialists in Household Linen, Carpets, Linoleum, Welsh Flannels, etc., etc.

Established before the advent of the Cambrian or Manchester and Milford Railways.

This firm is noted for quality and reasonable charges.

## THE WELSH STORES
### ABERYSTWYTH

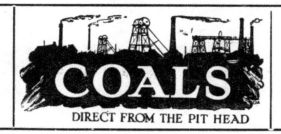

# The New Model Laundry
## BATH STREET, ABERYSTWYTH

All Classes of Laundry Work undertaken and treated with the utmost care. The very latest and up-to-date machinery and only the best workmanship.

COLLECTION AND DELIVERY BY MOTOR VANS.

# Public Swimming Baths
## BATH STREET

MIXED BATHING, :: HOT SALT BATHS A SPECIALITY.

Fresh Sea Water pumped Daily. Swimming Instructor in Attendance. :: Bath 72ft. x 30ft.

*Open from 8 a.m. to 8 p.m. :: Sundays 7 to 11 a.m.*

# The Imperial Cinema
## BATH STREET

*BEST AND LATEST PICTURES.*

*Projection Perfect.*

Continuous from 6 p.m. to 11 p.m. :: Matinee Daily if wet—11.30 a.m. and 2.30 p.m. :: Full Orchestra.

# NEWEST BATHING MACHINES
On Beach.

(MIXED BATHING) where every care is taken.

*Proprietor—W. EVANS, Offices: Bath Street.*

'Phone 70.                                   Established 1885.

# The Centre for Coal.

# J. Jenkin Jones & Co.

## COAL MERCHANTS AND CONTRACTORS

**ONE PRICE—**
The Cheapest.

**ONE QUALITY—**
The Best.

*Your kind enquiries are solicited for all Coals. We shall be pleased to Quote for any quantity.*

*GIVE US A TRIAL.*

All kinds of Haulage work undertaken.

Our Motor Lorries deliver to all parts of the Country.

# ABERYSTWYTH

141

# Shopping Guide and Index to Advertisements.

ooooooOOoooooo

142

Views of Royal Pier Pavilion (see opposite.)

# Royal Pier Pavilion

## ORCHESTRAL CONCERTS

On the Pier every Morning and Afternoon (or in the Pavilion during inclement weather).

## SELECTED PICTURES

in the most comfortable and beautiful Hall in Wales—daily.

## THE CAFÉ

A kaleidoscope of colour, overlooking the Bay; is the coolest place in Town. Our Teas, Ices, and Iced Drinks from our Soda Fountains are unsurpassed.

## SALOON BAR

Fully Licensed.

## SACRED CONCERTS

Every Sunday during the Season.

CPSIA information can be obtained
at www.ICGtesting.com
Printed in the USA
BVHW031811191121
622071BV00002B/45

9 780992 734633